BasSketball

Lessons

22 Winning Principles For Youth Who Play Sports

Brent Bass

www.BasSketballLessons.com

BasSketball Lessons

Copyright © 2020 by Brent Bass

First Edition

ISBN: 978-1-73-416240-0

Here's what readers are saying about BasSketball Lessons

"BasSketball Lessons is right on time! Today, youth face frequent challenges and questions regarding who to turn to and trust on and particularly off the court. This book provides invaluable guidance to help them overcome obstacles they will certainly experience.

- Jamie F. Marcus, Former middle and high school Athletic Director/ Owner of Athletic Resource Management Associates, L.L.C.

"This book integrates fundamentals to succeed in basketball along with teaching valuable life skills and lessons. It helps develop a foundation for building future leaders on and off the court."

- Dell Robinson, Executive, Spelman-Johnson, Athletics Consulting / Former Commissioner, Great Lakes Athletic Conference.

****

As a way of saying thanks for purchasing BasSketball Lessons, I'd like to offer you the **FREE** opportunity to peek into the Audiobook.

With this offer you will receive both the book introduction, and a featured chapter, just go to www.**BasSketballLessons.com** and provide your information, to get the free offer right away!

Please know that the paperback and E-book versions of BasSketball Lessons is interactive. These versions will provide the reader with the chance to use their phone, tablet or other device to scan the QR code (see below) to hear and/or save the emphasized theme in each chapter.

Please take two of minutes to download a Free QR code reader application and try it.

Acknowledgements

I want to thank God, our Creator... He continues to provide me with everything I need. This includes great friends, some foes, and varied life experiences that have assisted in my continual growth.

I am grateful to my wife and kids, Sylvia, Brent Jr., Brandon, and Bradlee, for providing me with quiet time to just think, be and write. I thank my mother, father, sister, brothers and other family members for innumerable experiences that have shaped me.

I'd like to recognize, my friend Falecia Gibson, my writing coach Claudette Freeman, and once again, my wife for nudging me forward, editing and providing me with invaluable feedback. They helped ensure this book will appeal to youth and young adults and will be supportive to parents who are raising them to be focused and driven individuals.

I also want to thank my launch team which includes Wayne Bass, Nicole Sharpe, Pierre Turner, Mary Ellen Betterton, Michelle Victoria-Bellard, Fabio Amendola, Karen Ford, Leroy Tart, Rick Smith, Pat White and Aliastair Henry for helping to catapult this book forward.

I'd finally like to thank the game of basketball. Playing this sport recreationally and most of all, competitively, has allowed me to learn and grow under the tutelage of many knowledgeable coaches and mentors and also to commune personally with God, during my individual practices. This amazing game taught me to take risks, to lead, and so many other valuable lessons I may not have experienced otherwise.

Preface

Love at first swish

*"When I saw you I fell in love,
and you smiled because you knew."*
Arrigo Boito, Italian poet

The dark green plastic toy soldiers shooting at each other on the bleachers could not hold my attention any longer as I suddenly heard the screams of the crowd and saw blurs of people in red and white running back and forth. Whatever was happening, it was great to see the reactions of my parents every time the ball passed through that orange thing. "What is this?" is what I likely asked myself at three years of age. All I know is that whatever was happening encapsulated me; my toy soldiers had to cease fire for a few minutes.

From the earliest stage of my life, all I remember is basketball – all day, every day, game after game, and year upon year. I was continually exposed to watching people run and shoot this burnt orange thing that seemed to be so important to everybody.

The most notable person I saw people cheer excitedly for time and time again was my brother Kevin, or "Fish," as they knew him throughout the New York City region. His daily or weekly accomplishments on the court were incredible, from what I could understand.

From age four to eight, Iona College was a basketball incubator for me. I remember excitedly running to the top of the bleachers and watching game after game as Kevin showcased his talent, and I watched intently, with my toy soldiers in tow, and amazingly saw him become the all-time leading scorer there.

At about seven years of age, I remember watching him play at the Mecca of basketball, Madison Square Garden, against the University of North Carolina at Charlotte and the great Cedric "Cornbread" Maxwell. I also remember feeling the hoopla surrounding the game against St. John's University, coached by the legendary Lou Carnesecca at Iona's Mulcahy Center, in which Iona prevailed. I also will never forget the game when I was at my favorite spot, at the top of the bleachers at Iona, when he got a steal. As he ran the length of the court to lay it in, just as he jumped, all the lights went out and it went pitch black. Wow! I have no clue who won or lost this game, but this experience made an indelible imprint within my mind.

After games at Iona, we'd say goodbye to my brother - who would have to put down his headphones from his interview - then we'd rush to get into the Chevy Impala or green Chevy station wagon that smelled like fish (because my father loved fishing), and turn to WFAS-radio and listen to Pat Digilio talk about how the Gaels did and what another great performance "Fish" produced, as my father drove us home.

Not only do I remember the games, I remember going to the locker room and being greeted by all the great guys on that team that included Dave Budd, Ray Hyland, Glen Vickers, Dennis Bange, Kevin Manderville, Dave Brown, Lester George, Cedric Cannon, Kevin Hamilton and the other guys who made me feel welcomed.

The compilation of my earliest basketball experiences gave me no choice but to have hoop dreams. It became part of my DNA and I knew I had to be a part of the smells, the sights, and the conversations surrounding basketball. My prayer was that I would thrill the crowd one day and have camaraderie with teammates like this.

After Kevin graduated, he had the opportunity to try out and play professional basketball. He didn't make it and I remember being pretty upset about it. He bounced back with his great education and transferred the principles he learned in sports to the business world, where he went on to become a top salesman at IBM.

I soon transferred my love of watching Kevin play to watching games all day on television. One of my favorite players was always on. On any given night, I could watch Alex English, Dan Issel, David Thompson, George "Iceman" Gervin, Lary Bird, Magic Johnson, James Worthy, Kareem Abdul Jabbar, Mo Cheeks or Dr. J. If I wasn't watching my favorites, I was shooting or playing ball in my backyard, heading to Massaro Park or tagging along with my brother, Wayne, to his high school basketball practices.

As I grew into my pre-teens and teens, I was still mesmerized by basketball. Wayne Anderson, one of my friends, would always ring the doorbell and ask me if I was going to the school party on Fridays. Inevitably the answer was no, as I'd return to the black and white grainy television in my room to watch NBA or college basketball, while my brother Wayne whipped up the best Vanilla Milkshakes for us to devour.

Emulating the success of my brother and my favorite players was all that was on my mind, all the time. Not only did I want to emulate the memories I had of my brother on the court, but off it as well. His humor, charm, service, and grace towards others were effortless and selfless. I was listening and learning from the best about what to do and what not to do firsthand!

The valuable lessons and principles I learned from my brother on and off the court and the seamless association with basketball was very beneficial for me. The lessons were reinforced by a strong village of people that undoubtedly cared for me. They included my parents, my brother Wayne, sister Leslie, our neighbors, my cousin Pierre, my coach Vincent Smith, my first youth basketball coaches Wilbur Bartley and Clyde Hilliard, youth baseball coach Danny Lupe, youth football coach Mark Murray, my high school basketball coach Mike DelVal, my college coaches Eddie Fogler and John Thurston and all of my high school and college teammates and friends with whom I experienced life with. They all taught me priceless life lessons, some of which I will share in this book.

Table of Contents

Acknowledgements

Preface

LESSONS:

The Eye of the Tiger

"The future never takes care of itself; it is taken care of, shaped, molded, and colored by the present. Our todays are what our yesterdays made them; our tomorrows must inevitably be the product of our todays."

Dennis Kimbro, American best-selling author,
master trainer and college professor

Staggeringly tired, drenched in sweat, during or after shooting the three hundredth jump shot of the day at Rumbrook Park on Saturday mornings, I would invariably hear, "You have to have the eye of the Tiger!"

Kevin, my in-family coach, knew from experience that if I didn't have the focus and drive, I could be pulled away from accomplishing my goal by other distractions. He told me that successful players learn how to concentrate their minds and become the best because they have a target. A target that is like the prey a tiger sees when he's hungry. Once he puts his eyes and mind on securing his food, he ignores every distraction and pursues it with great intensity.

Having the "eye of the tiger" is the reason I made the decision to focus only on basketball after my sophomore year of high school. I realized I could concentrate my mind, my attitude, and my effort to create habits and skills to develop into a player worthy of obtaining a scholarship at the Division One level, which was my target. I understood if I could keep my attention from being diverted, I could gain an edge on others who also wanted a scholarship, but didn't have the focus.

I began to invest long hours of practice to get better. I practiced dribbling and lifted weights in my basement after the sun went down. I also developed the habit of getting up early to go to the park, before school, to shoot a couple hundred jump shots, while my competition was sleeping!

Don't be fooled into believing that if you simply emulate your favorite NBA players or YouTube athletes for a few minutes prior to your game, that you'll play just like them and college coaches will beat down your door. In order to play at the Division One level (or any collegiate level) it takes the development of a strong work ethic to go along with thousands of hours of practice. Once this work ethic is developed, it can also help to carry you forward in your life after sports.

After your playing career ends and you pursue opportunities in other areas such as business, politics, medicine or education, you will know and understand the sacrifice that is required to become excellent off the court also.

I remember one day in ninth grade, looking at the large map of the United States that hung on the wall in my room. I estimated there must be hundreds of thousands of athletes across the states playing high school basketball who would like to play college basketball like me. I contemplated, after learning there were approximately 300 Division One Basketball institutions across the United States, if I could be in the top 300 players after my junior year and as I became a rising senior in high school, I could put myself in the position to get one of the limited and valuable scholarships at one of these colleges. Soon thereafter, my determination soared.

I also thought about an assignment given in school, in which I was to write everything done during every hour of the week. At the end of the assignment, I realized that I wasted two to three hours every day doing meaningless activities like watching silly television shows, socializing or doing other things, rather than working toward my goal. I understood if I managed my time better I'd prepare myself to realistically compete for a scholarship.

Having and keeping the "eye of the tiger" is a daunting challenge. Life has become much more complicated than when I was a kid. Today, student-athletes manage playing sports and other real-life responsibilities, like school work, taking care of younger siblings, working part-time jobs, peer pressure in addition to managing social media profiles, video games, phone alerts, and raging hormones all at the same time.

The good news is, if you closely analyze your time and are able to manage or eliminate things that are unnecessary, which likely consist of excuses and distractions, and decide to work hard with consistency and balance, you may reach your dream faster than you realize. However, thankfully this principle can be applied to other areas of life, whether it is in sports, education, business or other endeavors. In life, once you have your eye on the target, learn to maintain your focus and you are bound to catch the prey.

Let your eyes look straight ahead;
fix your gaze directly before you.

Give careful thought to the paths
for your feet and be steadfast in all your ways.
Do not turn to the right or the left;
keep your foot from evil.
Proverbs 4:25-27

Scan the QR code below to hear and save
the emphasized theme in this chapter.

Everything is a test

"Holding on to hope when everything is dark,
is the greatest test of faith."
Yasmin Mogahed, International speaker and author

Kevin would always say, "Everything is a test." He would declare that trouble comes into your life to see how you will react to them and to examine how committed you are to reaching the goal.

He maintained that a test or trial can be as simple as lying in bed until noon, hanging out on the corner with the guys or watching television when you know you should be shooting three hundred jump shots every morning, doing dribbling drills, studying for an exam, doing your homework or even preparing for a job interview.

We are all tested daily. The decisions you make on a daily basis can affect your life. This is comparable to a driver who must make a choice when they reach a fork in the road; you have the option to pick one direction or the other. Your responsibility is to contemplate or even seek counsel on the best direction to go and to choose the one that will provide the most positive outcome.

Unfortunately, regardless of the decisions you make, some will take you down a rocky and hard road; however, if you can keep the end goal in mind, you will gain valuable experience.

As a student-athlete, my challenge was developing discipline to get better every day, instead of spending time doing unrelated activities or resting excessively. I had to strengthen my body as well as my mind in order to train in the early morning and evening hours, while others rested in season and out of season.

In college, the trial was developing the fortitude to keep my basketball goals in mind while also working hard to get my degree, maintaining my relationships and keeping a good attitude while not playing as much as I would have liked to at Wichita State.

Although the decisions you make during a test seem menial when you are young, they can be rather impactful and sometimes have lifelong consequences. Circumstances at any moment may be tough for you. You could have family or friends pushing you to be better in new ways or you may be experiencing things in life you are not sure about. I know it can be grueling mentally, physically, emotionally and educationally. If you keep the positive goal in mind and work, you'll make progress toward it day by day.

I always talk with students in my health class about the tests they will encounter as it relates to trying drugs, smoking/vaping, drinking alcohol, and having sex. I tell them that although you may be enticed to try many of these things, the consequences of the action, even just one time, can lead to a lifetime of pain, addiction or even death. That advice is true for you as well; thus, you should make the more healthful solution when confronted with one of these.

Ultimately, you will grasp that mistakes happen, and you won't prevail in every challenge; however, as I've heard televangelist Joyce Meyer state: "As you take and pass more tests, you'll eventually be promoted just as you are advanced to the next grade every school year".

Think wise; I heard Steve Harvey, the popular comedian, state that without a test you would never have a testimony to share with others on how the decisions, practice, prayers, dedication, sacrifice and focus all pay off for you, eventually, on your life journey.

Count it all joy, my brothers,
when you meet trials of various kinds,
for you know the testing of your faith
produces steadfastness.
and let steadfastness have its full effect,
that you may be perfect and complete,
lacking in nothing.
James 1:2-4

Scan the QR code below to hear and save
the highlighted message in this chapter.

You are qualified

"There are people less qualified than you
doing the things you want to do
simply because they decided to believe in themselves.
Period."
Anonymous

The famous civil rights leader, Rev. Jesse Jackson used to assert: "You are qualified! You are qualified!" He would chant the affirmation over and over to the crowds he spoke to, because, I believe, he felt some people thought they could not measure up to the everyday challenges society threw at them.

During my teen years, Kevin would from time to time declare: "Never forget, you are qualified bro!" He infused this into my psyche, knowing faith and confidence were necessary for me to reach my dream of playing college basketball.

In my travels, running youth athletic programs and in school settings, I have met many kids and adults who underachieve and never reach their full potential. They never reach their full ability because they lack confidence and vision, and feel they are not qualified to attain various goals.

Unfortunately, you will never build self-confidence if you don't do something more than what you've already done or accomplished. This is due to fear. Fear as defined in Webster's dictionary is "being afraid of someone or something as likely to be dangerous, painful, or threatening."

When you are fearful, you step back from the front of the line and let others dazzle in roles that you could rightfully play. You will observe, admire, and envy others operating in their ability and authority, not recognizing this person likely struggled with their own self-confidence, but fought through the fear to advance. You tend to only see the end result, not the struggle.

To feel better about your fearful or unqualified condition, sometimes you use excuses or perhaps blame your teachers, friends, weather, food, genetics, boredom, and the lack of time.

To overcome the fear of being unqualified and stepping into knowing you are qualified, you must first wake-up and recognize playing the victim never works. Then you must create the desire to change your mindset and develop confidence by taking calculated risks into the unknown.

Instead of claiming: "I can never get an A in one of your classes because I have to give a presentation;" you can assert: "You know what, I can overcome my fear by listening and learning all I can in class and practice as long as it takes, so I can present my best work authentically." Instead of proclaiming: "I will never be able to lose weight. I just love to eat too much;" declare: "I will lose this weight; I'll research and try every way possible to get healthier."

Do not resign yourself to mediocrity by consistently focusing on what you don't have. Instead, focus on what you can do, what you do have, and the strengths that you can improve upon.

Did you know that Michael Jordan, the greatest basketball player to grace the planet, was once cut from his High School basketball team in 10th grade? However, after that, he worked hard to improve his game to make the team the next year and the rest is history. Had Mr. Jordan just sulked, gave up or simply blamed the coach, his teachers, his mom or the fact that he didn't have a hoop in the backyard, he would have never garnered legions of adoring fans and the billionaire status he claims now.

When you stop playing the victim in any area of life, it can be like acquiring the skill to walk all over again. You can never know what to expect and it can be terrifying as you may fall, but it's worth it. Even if you fall, you can get back up and try again and again.

For me, hosting a podcast called "Be Grateful Anyway," starting a family business and writing this book are examples of moving from the state of fear and feeling unqualified to one of freedom, and being absolutely qualified to offer more to the world than comfortable past accomplishments.

For 35 years, I thought about writing this book. I envisioned people would read it and I'd be able to speak to athletes about life skills, perseverance, and how to transfer skills from sports into success outside of athletics; however, having been an average writer, it didn't do much to boost my self-assurance. I felt totally unqualified. Eventually, I decided to take a leap of faith into unfamiliar territory and not allow the thief of procrastination, negative self-talk, victim thinking, and a lack of discipline to get me to quit.

I had to keep telling myself: I am qualified. I am capable. I am worthy!

You are qualified also! So, get to work.

"You are the light of the world.
A town built on a hill cannot be hidden.
Neither do people light a lamp and put it under a bowl.
Instead, they put it on its stand,
and it gives light to everyone in the house.
In the same way,
let your light shine before others,
that they may see your good deeds
and glorify your Father in heaven.
Matthew 5:14-16

Scan the QR code below to hear and save the emphasized theme in this chapter.

Detours are inevitable

"Let's face it, life is a constant challenge. It's full of unexpected detours that no one but you can navigate."
Sheryl Crow, American musician

The score was tied in the game against High Point College and I had the ball on the wing with seven seconds remaining on the clock. I jab stepped right, swung the ball through to the left against the defender, and drove baseline to get the last shot up before the buzzer sounded and I was fouled. The packed gym of 2000 went wild. At once, our coach, John Thurston, with his shirt frazzled, tie loosened, and face turning red, called a timeout.

So here I was, two free throws to shoot to secure the win with no time left and I walked over to the sideline with my teammates Troy Ebron, Ed Smith, Neil Willougby, and Marvin Work. Coach tries to compose himself. As I'm standing there considering the situation, I told myself: "Wow, well this is what you dreamed about!"

As I stood with my teammates, during the timeout, to discuss what I thought would be the strategy on the steps we should take if I made or missed the free throw attempts, coach began to tell a random story about the time he was a child and how much fun he had playing and chasing people around the playgrounds in the Bronx. It was very amusing! His comedy lightened the mood of an intense game and took my mind off potentially missing the free throws.

As I left the bench, I was snickering. Then I went to the free throw line and a referee handed me the rock. I took my first shot and it hit the bottom of the net. I got the ball again, went through my routine again and nailed the second shot! We won!

What a feeling! It was a dream come true. Finally, all I had ever imagined came into reality!

I've lived my dream of playing Division One college basketball at Wichita State University and playing in front of 10,000 people a night for two years, where I was a small fish on a campus with approximately twenty thousand other students and a city full of raving basketball fans.

I also had the opportunity to play and live out part of my dream at the Division Two level at an awesome school named Wingate College (now University). At Wingate, I was considered a slightly bigger fish in a smaller pond, as there were only about two thousand students on campus, but it was well-suited for me.

At Wichita State, basketball was not playing out as I had hoped. In my sophomore year, partly due to a serious ankle injury suffered late in the summer that lingered into the start of the season, I played a reduced role from my freshman year. With Basketball being the one thing that kept my mind off being fifteen hundred miles away from home, I was not happy with my role in a program on the upswing. I had to make a tough decision if I was to play the game I loved while being able to participate in a more meaningful role.

When I look back on my experience at both institutions,

although sometimes tough and depressing, I can declare I have no regrets about being a small fish or a big fish because I gave basketball my all in every workout, practice, and game. In fact, if I could do it all over again today, I'm not sure I'd change much.

I am extremely grateful to have had these experiences, because according to the NCAA, "Only two percent of all high school athletes will play sports at ANY college level." That is astounding! When you consider this, it means out of the 100 people you have played against in tournaments or at school, only two of you, on average, will ever go on to college on a scholarship!

As it pertains to becoming a pro, the NCAA statistics state: "FEWER than two percent of college student-athletes go on to be professionals. They further report that in reality, most student-athletes depend on academics to prepare them for life after college. Education is important. There are nearly half a million NCAA student-athletes, and most of them will become professionals in something other than sports."

When I get the opportunity to share my advice and experience with student-athletes, one of the things I'm often asked is where they should consider going to college to pursue their academic or athletic dreams.

Fortunately, I'm able to share my experience at both levels of college and discuss the pros and cons of each type of institution. In particular, I speak to what it is like to be one of the all state or nationally-recognized ballplayers on a large campus, but also what it is like to play a bigger athletic role at a smaller school where the competition is also tough, but not as widely recognized.

Ultimately, you should reach for the stars regardless of where you plan to go to school or what you decide to do with your life. It is very likely you will have to redefine what success means to you. If all success meant to me was becoming a professional player, I'd be lost. I have repositioned myself happily in sports by becoming a Parks and Recreation professional, sports business owner and Athletics Director.

As you move forward in life, remain flexible because you will hit detours, which means you must be prepared mentally and educationally after the ball stops bouncing. When this happens, after you've given your full dedication and time to school, sports, business, music or something else, at some point, you may have to re-adjust to reach new and different dreams.

"And we know that in all things
God works for the good of those who love him,
who have been called according to his purpose."
Romans 8:28

Scan the QR code below to hear and save
the highlighted message in this chapter.

15

Manage your time

"The bad news is time flies.
The good news is you're the pilot."
Michael Altshuler, Motivational Speaker

One 75-degree day in the park across from Lefrak City in Queens, NY, my youth basketball trainer, Vincent Smith, took his hat off and wiped the sweat from his brow, pulled me to the side and advised: "Listen Brent, you only have about 200 games between all the summer leagues, camps, and high school basketball to show that you can play on the next level, so you better keep working hard at improving your skills and getting good grades in school."

When I thought about it and looked around the court at Tim Baysmore, Carlos Perez, Lenny Boyce, and Kenny Anderson, and saw them working hard to achieve a similar dream, it moved me to work even harder to make each practice and game the best it could be.

Sometimes you need a wake-up call or to be reminded that time waits for no one. You must realize that you should make wise use of every second to be the best and work your hardest going forward. Coach Vince didn't want me to look back on my middle and high school years knowing I wasted any time by not working hard. He knew the time was, and always is, NOW to keep improving. That is a great lesson that applies to your life outside of sports also.

I know my children, Brent Jr. and my twin boys, Brandon and Bradlee, think they have unlimited time (at the time this book was written, they are 14 and 8, respectively). That timeless feeling is great while you are young and having fun all day, every day. I remember the feeling vividly. Once you get older or understand this lesson, you'll start to put more value on the time you have.

Willie Jolley, Author of The Minute Motivation, states:

> "Pennies create dollars, and minutes create hours,
> the difference is if we throw away pennies
> we can make more but time is not the same.
> We have a limit on the time we have on this earth."

Fortunately, every year, you have been gifted a birthday to celebrate, but to be honest, one day you won't.

I often think about Jason Harris (12), Winston Parks (20's), David Purdy (24) and Rodney Abrams (26) and a fifteen-year-old from my neighborhood who all died unexpectedly from things like not waking up from sleep or being hit by a car when crossing a street. I also think about the violence, which is so prevalent and takes place in supposedly safe elementary, middle, high schools, college campuses, and other environments. Do you think my friends or victims that died in any of these shootings knew it was their last day to live? These things happen to young people, just like you, every day.

You probably tell yourself, "It'll never happen to me." You may feel as if you are invincible because you are young, the star of the team, you are in good shape, and all the girls or guys are chasing after you. The reality is you never know what life has in store for you and this is something you must accept in order to live without fear or limits.

The good news is although you can never be sure how many remaining practices or games you have left to play, or the number of days, years or decades you have to live, you can, at any age, use the remaining time living in the moment and maximizing your time.

Yet you do not know what tomorrow will bring.
What is your life? For you are a mist that appears
for a little time and then vanishes.
James 4:14

Scan the QR code below to hear and save
the emphasized message in this chapter.

Do not quit

"Many of life's failures are people
who did not realize how close
they were to success when they gave up."
Thomas A. Edison, American inventor and businessman

Early one morning in October 1986, I was waiting at the light to cross 21st Street in Wichita, Kansas with my bicycle, to ride across campus to our four-a.m. basketball practice. The wind was whipping around; it was so cold, and I wasn't happy. I remember wondering to myself, "Why am I doing this?"

Here I was, thousands of miles from home, with no friends, waking up at three a.m. to make it to practice. I asked myself, "Am I crazy or are these coaches crazy?" Of course, I knew I would have to leave practice, go to my other classes until 1:30, eat lunch, head back to another practice again at 3:00, go to dinner and after eating, go to study hall until 8:00pm and then do it all over again, day after day. I wanted to quit because that was not the dream I envisioned.

I remember looking at the keychain my sister Leslie gave me that had a poem written by Edgar A. Guest on it.

> *"When things go wrong, as they sometimes will, when the road you're trudging seems all uphill, when the funds are low and the debts are high, and you want to*

19

smile, but you have to sigh, when care is pressing you down a bit, rest if you must, but don't you quit.

Life is queer with its twists and turns, as every one of us sometimes learns, and many a fellow turn about when he might have won had he stuck it out. Don't give up though the pace seems slow - You may succeed with another blow.

Often the goal is nearer than It seems to a faint and faltering man; Often the struggler has given up When he might have captured the victor's cup; And he learned too late when the night came down, how close he was to the golden crown.

Success is failure turned inside out - The silver tint in the clouds of doubt, and you never can tell how close you are, it might be near when it seems afar;

So, stick to the fight when you are hardest hit, it's when things seem worst that you must not quit."

Reading the poem gave me some solace that the sadness and concerns I had would turn for the better and wouldn't last forever. I had never experienced such drudgery and homesickness in my life. I was depressed.

Several weeks thereafter, I started to feel better as I became more acclimated to the schedule, and especially when four o'clock practices were abandoned. It also helped that the game season started; I created new friendships and developed a stronger bond with my new teammates off the court.

I'm glad I didn't quit.

As a coach and athletic administrator today, I, unfortunately, see student-athletes quit teams for the most menial of reasons. I've had conferences with parents and have witnessed kids quit teams because the coach ran them too hard in conditioning drills; the coach raised his voice; the team lost three games in a row, or they believed the coach was biased in favor of certain players. Sometimes it's simply a question of clashing personalities between players and coaches.

I will tell you, just as I tell my own sons and student-athletes, that just because things don't start off right, you should still give it your all in practice and see every activity through to the end of the season, trust the process and then re-evaluate it from there.

Often, I find my student-athletes and my children are pleased they kept their original commitment, as their playing time increases and as they develop stronger friendships with their teammates.

This is true for most things. You must give everything you do a justifiable amount of time to see what direction it is going before making a rash decision you may regret one day.

You never know, the person who is playing in front of you may (or may not) get hurt and open up minutes for you to play more. Injuries are a natural occurrence in sports. If the opportunity presents itself, it is meaningless if you are not prepared.

In many ways, sports can be used as a metaphor for life. Opportunities can also arise unexpectantly in the work environment. If any of these scenarios happen, the person who is able to take advantage of the opportunity can and will flourish. In essence, you want to be prepared to showcase your talent, if and when called upon.

Believe me, I know that it's tough to endure the losses; sit the bench; lift the weights; run the miles; do the schoolwork listen to a demanding teacher, parent, supervisor, sibling or coach. Despite the challenges, which can be tough to accept keep working toward your goal and you will eventually win Just don't give up too soon!

Let us not become weary in doing good,
for at the proper time
we will reap a harvest if we do not give up.
Galatians 6:9-12

Scan the QR code below to hear and save
the highlighted message in this chapter.

Take out the trash

"It is easier to build strong children
than to repair broken men."
Frederick Douglas, American abolitionist and orator

I can hear my mom yelling even now: "Brent, go downstairs and get me a grape soda!" Or, she'd yell: "Wayne, it's time to wash the dishes!" She would poke her head in the back door to yell: "I'm home," when she arrived with a car full of groceries. She would rattle off a list of chores we were asked to do or needed to do like put the groceries away, take out the trash, wash the dishes, get the laundry off the line or make our beds every day.

As teenagers, none of us were really happy to be taken away from our music, tv show or from playing our games in the backyard with our friends. But we learned quickly in the face of stern discipline, that being obedient to our parents first and foremost, along with our guardians, neighbors, coaches, teachers, and mentors, was very important.

My siblings and I would help with whatever our parents needed or wanted us to do because we were grateful for the groceries that filled the cupboard, for nice clothes to wear, and warm beds to sleep in.

We understood that helping around the house was the responsibility of all family members in order to be a full-fledged part of our household.   If we didn't grasp the need to vacuum, wash dishes, take out the trash or make our beds, how else would we have learned that these were important?

I am quite sure my parents knew that one day we'd have to leave home, take care of ourselves, and we had to be trained and disciplined to do these on our own.

Have you ever looked at animals in their natural state? Instinctually, once animals reach a certain milestone, they have to depart the home. For some, it is days; for others, weeks or years. In many cases, the pups must evolve quickly and grasp running, camouflaging and hunting for themselves because they will not thrive or survive if they don't. The same concept applies to humans. You will not blossom if you don't apply various life or coping skills you are being taught by your parents, teachers, coaches and eventually, perhaps even your boss.

Therefore, when you are asked to help at home, take a break, put down the phone, pause the video game and assist with groceries, shopping, washing dishes or vacuuming the house. Do these activities without an attitude, negative tone of voice, screwed up face or huffing and puffing. Perform these actions with gratitude and you will feel good about your contribution to the family.

Children, obey your parents in the Lord,
for this is right.
Honor your father and mother
which is the first commandment
with a promise so that it may go well with you
and that you may enjoy long life on the earth.
Ephesians 6 1-3

———————————▶

Scan the QR code below to hear and save
the emphasized theme in this chapter.

Go to class

"Just as God supernaturally opens doors,
He supernaturally closes doors.
If God closed it, He has something further in store."
Joel Osteen, American pastor and author

One of the most astounding things I gathered when I finally played and coached basketball at the intercollegiate level was that some teammates and players I coached did not take full advantage of having basketball to work for them but instead, they worked to play basketball.

What I mean is, some former teammates did not take full advantage of the free education that basketball offered them. A free education, for many, can be used as a ticket into a whole new world of unlimited opportunities. Opportunities that would not be available without the all-important college degree.

Some guys who were primarily focused on going pro, skipped classes and just showed up for basketball practice as if they were already paid athletes. If they did go to class, some took the instructional part of the free education casually and weren't concerned much with preparing for their Plan B.

It's unfortunate because just as the NCAA statistics I shared before indicated, NONE of my former teammates or players, from my knowledge, have moved on to play substantially on the professional level either in the United States or elsewhere.

When you land on a university campus as a student-athlete, in any sport, you realize quickly the competition is fierce to reach the pros. Many, unfortunately, never consider what happens if they just aren't good enough, get injured, and can no longer participate again. They failed to consider their future in the absence of sports.

As an athlete, even your best intentions don't always take you where you plan or hope. Inevitably there will come a time when your participation in sports will cease. What will you do then?

Rest assured, I believe with all my heart that even if you don't make the pros, there is life after sports. Remember, that NCAA statistics state, "more than 98% of all athletes will go pro in something other than sports."

When they say, "other than sports," it could, for you, mean working in sports in another capacity. I know people who have lucrative sports careers, other than playing. They are photographers, journalists, scouts, coaches, college professors, chefs, player personnel directors, general managers, sports information directors, ticket directors, conference commissioners, marketing directors, athletic directors, assistant athletic directors, player agents, owners and broadcasters.

Years ago, I would have never imagined that one day all the good and bad experiences I had playing sports would pour out of me and result in me being an author, offering advice, and speaking to you about dealing with issues in life. I believe putting my experiences in this format is what God intended for my life.

There is a plan for your life as well. To prepare for what, in all likelihood, will be next for you requires that you plan, have a good attitude, education, and faith to realize it.

For I know the plans I have for you,
declares the Lord,
plans for welfare and not for evil,
to give you a future and a hope.
Jeremiah 29:11

Scan the QR code below to hear and save the highlighted theme in this chapter.

Keep your word

"When you don't keep your word, you lose credibility."
Robin Sharma, Canadian writer

As an athletic director, I often ask student-athletes to help me out with menial tasks. Sometimes, I ask them to help with sweeping the court, getting the volleyball or basketball ball cart out of the closet, to open a locker room door or assist me in finding the latest hit songs on the sound system prior to games.

I remember once, I required assistance from a student-athlete to help in keeping score for a volleyball match. I asked him if he could aid me and he responded he could. As the start of the match approached and after checking in with him a couple of other times, I found him strolling out of the gym with his backpack on. I ran to him and inquired where he was going; he responded: "home." I asked him about his commitment. He shrugged his shoulders, laughed, and continued walking away.

Several months later, this same young man transferred schools, and I received a call from the District of Columbia Athletic Association asking if this fellow, was a decent kid and if I would recommend him as a student-athlete. It was unfortunate, but I was sincere about my feelings and my rapport with the young man, based on more than that one incident. Shortly thereafter, I heard he was not allowed to play his senior year. I don't know if he was not allowed to play because I didn't give him a glowing report. I am certain my message impacted him negatively, but it was the truth.

 The good news is ultimately this experience had a positive impact on his life.

A few years after his graduation from high school, he visited our school and walked over to me at a basketball game, shook my hand and whispered, "Hey Mr. Bass, I just want to express my thanks to you". I responded: "For what?" He commented: "For the lesson you taught me about keeping my word." I acknowledged the change, "I'm glad you finally got the lesson I tried to get through to you over and over." He nodded in approval, we shook hands and continued watching the game.

To my dismay, I continue to witness youth who burn bridges like this. For instance, instructors tell students they are available to tutor them after school and they never show up even though they make an appointment. I've seen some students laugh or yell at teachers, disrespecting them, not cognizant that they are exemplifying a lack of character, which could pose problems for them in future endeavors. Other students are what I call, "consistently inconsistent," meaning sometimes they show up for appointments, practices, games and just come and go with no reasonable excuse! Fortunately, and sometimes regrettably, these poor attitudes and behaviors become teachable moments, like it was for my former student-athlete.

You must begin to understand early on that adults don't easily forget the impressions made on them, particularly when the same behavior shows up repeatedly. Developing trust by consistently keeping your word and by maintaining a good attitude with people is crucial to your growth and can be impactful for those following in your footsteps.

Let me explain:

I remember when I entered middle school as a seventh grader. Mr. Kopicki, a Geometry Teacher, stopped me on the first day of school near the bottom of the steps next to his classroom and uttered: "You have to be a Bass." I smiled and replied: "Yes I am." I'm sure he recognized the family resemblance. As the youngest of four children, it was common for me to be greeted nicely. I discovered by this time, that I was a beneficiary of the power of the positive association with my siblings. I was given the benefit of the doubt that I was a "good kid," before even meeting people.

Yes, some people hated on me or teased me subtlety for being "such a nice kid," but I realized it was because they were envious of the influence I possessed, based upon my associations.

I cannot over emphasize the importance of keeping your word, associating with positive people, and how creating and maintaining positive relationships with friends, coaches, administrators, family members, and counselors is essential. These are attributes that will undoubtedly help you to build a successful future for yourself and also for your family and those associated with you.

When a man makes a vow to the Lord or takes an oath
to obligate himself by a pledge,
he must not break his word

but must do everything he said.
Numbers 30:2

Scan the QR code below to hear and save
the emphasized theme in this chapter.

Just because

"The best feeling of happiness is when you're
happy because you made someone else happy."
Anonymous

My sons and I were at the gym and set up a 3-on-3
basketball game with two other fellows. As we started
the game, I noticed a dad and son stopped their serious
workout to watch us as we played. I asked them if they
wanted to join. They jumped at the chance to take part in
the game.

One of the reasons, I asked them to join us was because I
felt it was a good opportunity to demonstrate a spirit of
inclusion to my kids, and also because we were there just to
have fun.

We played a couple of enjoyable games and afterwards, I
asked the dad why they were working out. He mentioned his
son needed to build confidence in basketball because he was
a baseball player and really wanted to make the basketball
team at this high school, and tryouts were starting soon.

I asked him if I could talk with his son. He said "Sure," and
he moved about 25 feet away. I gave his son tips on what
coaches look for and the small things he could do to set
himself apart from the more experienced players and peers

who were trying out with him. I told him that the key was to keep a positive mindset, to be coachable by doing whatever the coach required, to never take his eyes off the coach when he's talking or giving instructions, and to ask questions if necessary.

His father nodded in approval as I spoke and thanked me as we left.

I believe we all can serve others when the opportunity presents itself. I am experienced in this area and I considered helping this young man to be my obligation.

For most of us, including you, even you can assist others daily by:

- Opening and holding the door for others;

- Greeting people with a nice hello;

- Simply smiling genuinely at others;

- Looking to help people, who need help carrying objects or who need assistance on slippery sidewalks.

These are just a few of the things you can do just because the opportunity presents itself.

Unfortunately, with the growth of social media, I have seen people instead pull out their phones to record harmful incidents such as fights in school, and watching people get hit by flying objects when it would be more appropriate to warn the person of the impending danger.

There is something seriously wrong with this mindset. It is a spirit of selfishness rather than service. Life is not all about the bloopers you see weekly on television or that you and others post on social media to get more "likes".

As student-athletes and leaders, you should familiarize yourself with helping others for no reason at all. The positive benefits you will get from helping someone with no benefit to yourself will last in your heart much longer than by knowingly watching an elderly lady fall over a curb and get hurt.

Additionally, you set a good example to other students about your character, what you care about and how they should themselves act if presented with a similar opportunity.

The best benefits of assisting others are the good feelings you will feel in your heart. Additionally, sometimes those you support will reciprocate their appreciation with a simple thank you, a monetary tip, or even an offer to help you some way in return.

'For I was hungry, and you gave me something to eat,
I was thirsty and you gave me something to drink,
I was a stranger and you invited me in,
I needed clothes and you clothed me,
I was sick and you looked after me,
I was in prison and you came to visit me.'
Matthew 25:35-40

Scan the QR code below to hear and save the highlighted message in this chapter.

If you are on time, you are late

"If you are five minutes early,
you are already ten minutes late."
Vince Lombardi, American football player and coach

One night during my freshman year at Wichita State, I strolled into my dorm room and found my roommate, Joe Griffin, asleep. I noticed he had his ankles wrapped with white athletic tape, as if basketball practice started in a few minutes, although we had recently finished that day's practice, ate dinner and had study hall that evening. I chuckled to myself and wondered why he was still fully taped, as I strode to my side of the suite to relax.

Upon waking up the next day, I took a shower and when I walked out, Joe was awake. I proclaimed to him: "You are hilarious!" He countered "Why, do you say that, B?" I answered because you slept with your ankles wrapped. He exclaimed: "If Eddie! (our head coach) requires us to get our ankles wrapped more than an hour before practice, I'll be already taped. Is Eddie crazy? I am not going to the arena everyday by 2 pm for a 3:30 practice, I have better stuff to do!" I roared with laughter so hard, my stomach hurt. I then calmed myself, went to class, and waited to see what would happen later.

That afternoon, prior to practice, most of the team was in the locker room dressed for practice and being amused as our teammate, Lew Hill, sang Janet Jackson's song "Control," and here comes Joe, slowly strolling into the locker room with two senior players. He was a cool as a cucumber, wearing his sunglasses along with his Maroon Argo high school jacket that had the collar popped up. Joe quickly put on his practice gear, without seeing the athletic trainers, to get the required taping and sat down waiting for the coaches to arrive to watch film. Unfortunately for him, the medical team already told the coaches he missed his taping appointment and one coach poked his head in the room and asked Joe to come to the hallway.

We all looked at each other and knew it was trouble for him. Practice took place as normal. Unfortunately for Joe, he paid the price for his poor judgement. The coaches ran him so much after practice, we all felt sorry for him as we looked back and left the arena for dinner. He never missed getting freshly taped at the prescribed time again!

Joe had a genuine issue with the lesson on punctuality we were being taught. Many of the things the coaches asked us to do seemed unnecessary, but if there was one message we understood, it was that it's important to be on time.

With experience, you will also understand that the first impression that you leave on others is a lasting impression. Recognize that being late to appointments, classes, practices, and even job interviews can hurt you more than help. This is especially true when it comes to getting the extra help, promotion or opportunity that you seek.

As I mentioned in an earlier chapter, you will face competition for opportunities for advancement and you don't want to exclude yourself from those opportunities because you don't manage time well, but others you compete with, do.

Finally, I want to let you know that showing up at 2:55 for a 3:00 meeting is not prescribed. Being prompt means arriving, at the very least, fifteen minutes prior to your appointment. When you do so, you have the opportunity to do something like rehearse what you want to say, add emphasis to your pitch, study your notes or even relax so you can be your best self.

The plans of the diligent lead to profit
as surely as haste leads to poverty.
Proverbs 21:5

Scan the QR code below to hear and save
the emphasized theme in this chapter.

Should have, would have, could have

"Ninety-nine percent of the failures come from people
who have the habit of making excuses."
George Washington Carver, American scientist and inventor

My friend, Kent Jones, would refer to our family barbecue year after year, as "the Bass Famous." At the family barbeque, I would sit around with my friends, my siblings' friends, and older adults and laugh, listen, eat and nod my head to the thumping music in the background. I could feel the love and smell the aroma of the meats being cooked by my dad as the backyard filled up with friends and family.

One thing I always loved to hear at these yearly events were the tales of fun times in the past and present and listen to what people planned for their lives. What I began to realize from these stories, year after year, were people, who would often claim they should do this, they would do that but, or they could do something - if.

I realized, in many cases, these people, who were often the loudest in the yard, could only talk the talk. All they did was set the stage and get on a platform to amuse us at the barbecue. These are likely the same people who you meet on the corner, in the school lunchroom or some party. They blare about their wild tales of future success writing, singing designing, franchising, running marathons or other endeavors – "one day." It occurred to me then, and I note it now, that these are the folks who, in most cases, don't take a step towards achieving the professed goal they share. They are all talk and no work.

Here are some reasons I believe they are all talk:

1. They think it is easy to do what they profess and don't realize the demanding work it will take to reach the goal. Once they start, they don't have perseverance and give up;

2. They put the work off or procrastinate and remark they'll do it later, but later turns into never;

3. They eventually lose their health or die and can no longer pursue it;

4. They never had a dream in the first place.

In life, you must recognize that you are blessed to live each day and it should be used to work on your dream, whether you've talked about it publicly or not.

Do you know from the time you are born until you are 18 years old, there are only 936 weeks of living? If you are going to college, it's only a short time before you will likely leave home! If you are 14 years of age as you read this, you have lived 728 weeks! It's time to stop talking and get to work!

Do you want to look back at your life, sigh and think - I could have done this, I should have done that while I was young, or I would have done something if I used my time better?

No one wants to have regret in life, although we all will feel sad about a decision we made here or there. You can comfort yourself by knowing, although you made mistakes, you used your time as effectively as you could.

The only thing you can control while you are still alive are the actions you take, the words you express, and the time you have right now to work on accomplishing your dreams.

Learn to put action behind the words you profess to others and don't waste another minute running off at the mouth. Know that your word is your bond, and it has energy! It is your truth and an honest representation of your intention. Never deceive yourself or others.

For the Spirit God gave us does not make us timid,
but gives us power, love and self-discipline.
2 Timothy 1:7

Scan the QR code below to hear and save
the highlighted message in this chapter.

41

Be Coachable

"If you did it once, you can do it again, only better!"
Anonymous

I remember huffing and puffing and looking closely to make sure my Converse Weapons touched the black baseline of the basketball court because I knew if I missed placing my foot on it, I'd have to run again. I quickly turned and sprinted to the opposite foul line which was the finish line as coach counted down the seconds, "Three, two, one."

"Whew, I made it!" I ran my fourth or fifth consecutive timed sprint in 24 seconds, and I was dead tired. We all were. Unfortunately, coach yelled, "Guards up!" That yell meant we were to run again, after the forwards and centers finished.

I turned to the managers, Dave Wetzel, Ty White, and Floyd Butler and asked them, with a wink, if I had any plus points. These were points you could use to get out of running if you accrued enough of them from the coaches when you made hustle plays, like diving on loose balls, encouraging teammates, and other intangibles. Floyd snickered "no." I had to run again.

Coach Rick Callahan excitedly screamed out that next we would run a "suicide," a fitting term, in 28 seconds. A tough feat after practicing for two hours and already running four timed sprints.

We lined up and ran and gave it our all. One guy didn't make it! All the fellas groaned and uttered expletives, knowing that when one person misses the time, we all had to run again.

And so, we ran again and thankfully made the time, barely. Practice concluded with us assembling together at center court with Coach Fogler to discuss the day's practice.

As we made a semi-circle in front of coach, with an upbeat attitude, he remarked, "Guys, you see how you were able to make the time when you were tired? I want you to know that once you demonstrate you can make the time and even make the correct decisions in practice one time, I expect you can do it all the time. There are no excuses for not giving it your all from that point on."

While his moment of encouragement didn't supply much solace for us, as guys grimaced at others on the other side of the circle, it was a lesson well learned.

I've worked with many student-athletes and taught this same principle to players who needed modification of various skills such as shooting. We would work together and make successful necessary adjustments, but in many cases upon looking away and then glancing back, would see some of them reverting to old habits, resulting in them missing more shots than they make. While others who focused and made changes, regardless of whether someone was watching them or not, grew the fastest and improved steadily. I don't believe it was necessarily because the concepts were harder, they simply refused to be coached. The ultimate question is, are you coachable?

As you move ahead in life and whether you are on the court, in the classroom or at a job, one of the most important things you can do is eliminate distractions, work hard, and remain coachable after receiving correction or discipline from a parent, coach, supervisor, mentor and even God. Once you are able to listen and make the necessary changes, you can then duplicate and improve upon the success you've demonstrated and go to the next level, using this same principle repeatedly throughout life.

Whatever you do, work at it with all your heart,
as working for the Lord, not for men.
Colossians 3:23

Scan the QR code below to hear and save
the emphasized theme in this chapter.

Listen Learn Apply

"When you talk, you are only repeating
what you already know;
But when you listen, you may learn something new."
Dalai Lama, Tibetan spiritual leader

It was Thursday. I was about ten years of age and I was excited because it was steak night!

I recall eating my sirloin at the kitchen table. It must have been about 85 or 90 degrees because it was hot and muggy. Since we didn't have air condition in that room, my mom had the old green counter fan - that no longer had a screen on it to protect anyone from getting their fingers cut off - blowing on us as we ate, talked, and listened to the news on television.

I watched as Kevin voraciously ate a plate of greens first, and next, devoured his steak. The subject of school came up and I remember hearing him state that he wished he had kept going to college after college. I asked: "What do you mean, college after college?" He explained he wished instead of going from college to the working world, he would've gone on to get his master's degree.

I had no clue what a master's degree was, but I made a mental note that if he regretted it, I didn't want to make a similar mistake. It was also impactful because it was one of the first times I ever heard him express regret.

On another occasion, my father came home from work one night and when I opened the door for him, he immediately asked me: "What is that?" I asked: "What?" He answered "That smell. Have you been drinking?" I lied and muttered "No". He refuted: "Yes, you were." I then admitted that I had a taste of a beer and of course, blamed it on my sibling Wayne and his friend Jimmy Wilcox.

My father, who never talked a great deal, went on to declare that drinking alcohol was not good, and explained that he struggled with controlling a desire and taste for it and I should never do it again. I remember expressing my sorrow and mumbled a "yes sir" before vowing never to do it again. Of course, I made a mental note not to ever make a mistake like this again, based upon his insight.

I listened and understood from both the casual and serious conversations with Kevin and my father, to learn from the wisdom they shared. I made it part of my life plan and decided to capitalize on this knowledge, just as I hope my sons do by observing and listening to me.

From Kevin, I discerned the discontinuation of your education just to make money or to relax after either high school or college can make it much more difficult to get back into a routine of growing and studying in a school environment. I also learned that if you are able to continue with it, particularly a free opportunity, you should take advantage of it.

From my father, I gathered that not even one small taste of alcohol, drugs or smoking (vaping) for pleasure, or to avoid dealing with problems, is the answer. These things can lead to a lifetime of potentially dealing with serious mental, physical, or emotional consequences and regret.

The message from my father was particularly insightful because although he never talked much, I admired him greatly and had we not have had that brief conversation, alcohol could have potentially become a vice for me as well.

Based upon these instances, that I kept in the forefront of my mind, I sought opportunities for an advanced degree prior to completing my bachelor's degree, and only drink a couple of beers or a glass or two of wine a month. I have never smoked or done drugs.

Pay attention and listen carefully to the genuine words and actions of others. You'll begin to discern flaws and create strategies that you can use to your advantage and in various areas of life.

My dear brothers and sisters, take note of this:
Everyone should be quick to listen,
slow to speak and slow to become angry.
James 1:19

Scan the QR code below to hear and save the highlighted message in this chapter.

47

Show Respect

*"Show respect to people who don't even deserve it;
not as a reflection of their character,
but as a reflection of yours."*
Dave Willis, American voice actor and writer

Someone yelled, "Yo, Bass!" I started to turn around, but kept stepping. "Yo, Bass! Yo, Bass! I know you hear me! Forget you!" That's what I heard from some young knucklehead, as I kept walking down the hallway to the copier. Once I made my copies and headed back toward my office, the young man who was yelling for me said: "Hey Bass, I was calling you. Why didn't you turn around?" I was silent for a few seconds and looked at him quizzically, as I normally do. He asked me the question again, and I looked at him soberly as I've done to my students on many occasions. Then he muttered, "Oh, I'm sorry! Coach Bass, can you help me out by providing shorts for me to wear at practice today?"

I exclaimed, "Sure!" Then went on to explain, "Young man, I just want to reiterate to you that I don't hear too well when people address me disrespectfully." I normally would have gone on to correct him, reminding him that he can call me Coach or Mr. Bass and that's it, not by my first name or my last name only.

I may be old school, but I've been taught the correct way to address people who have seen, heard, and experienced life long before you and who are not in your peer group is by referring to them as Mr. or Ms. at the very least.

Webster's Dictionary defines respect as a feeling, understanding or acknowledgement that someone or something is important, serious, etc., and should be treated in an appropriate manner. Therefore, those who have paved the way in the past for our current and future success should be respected!

I recall when I was an athletic administrator at Eastern Michigan University in the late 1990's, I would often pick up the newspaper and read about a young local basketball phenom named LaVell Blanchard from Pioneer High school, only a few miles away in Ann Arbor. He was scoring 30 points a game, and was a highly sought-after athlete, and was being recruited by all the top Division One basketball programs.

One day, a local basketball trainer who I befriended, brought LaVell to a game and introduced me. I exclaimed, "Hi LaVell, I hear and read great things about you!" He responded: "Hello sir. Thank you, sir." With every yes and no question, he would respond with a yes sir or no sir. I was flabbergasted! I had never met such an articulate, humble, and respectful young man!

He left the same impression on anyone who met him. He was trained well in being respectful, as we all should be. I was not surprised that not long after I met him, Lavell won the National Gatorade Player of the Year award!

My advice to you is that greeting someone, such as LaVell did, by using a respectful term such as Coach, Mr., Ms., Sir or Ma'am is an important thing to do. Also, answering questions as he did with sir or ma'am on the end (genuinely and without sarcasm) is an absolute gesture you should always consider.

Do you want to be an Eagle who flies high or a chicken who stays grounded?

If you compare answering people this way to how most people greet or answer people nowadays, it is a far departure and will set you apart from your peers, and quite possibly, open doors for you that may not have been open otherwise, because of the impression you leave.

Coming up, I would have never thought about addressing Mr. Johnny Jones, a respected leader in my neighborhood, in Elmsford, NY with, "Hey, Johnny, how's it going my man?" Nor would I have said to my Social Studies Teacher, Mrs. Mary Lou Fiore, "What's up, Fiore?" They would have been incensed by this and there is no question my parents would have heard about it.

As a student-athlete, you must recognize that the respect you give will be the respect and appreciation you get back. Don't just straighten up and act or do the right thing when you are approaching the Coach or Athletic Director. They see past the façade already. Also, use good judgement and do not imitate many of your irresponsible peers, parents, teachers, local and even national leaders seen online or on television. This will hinder you more than help. Replicate only the actions and words of those you know and discern, in your heart, are doing the right thing.

With practice and focus, you will find it takes little effort to consistently show genuine and humble regard to ALL people. Your kind gestures, words, and addressing people properly and use of the words "Please and Thank you," are simple ways to leave a favorable impression on others. These may seem like insignificant things, but they really are important things in the grand scheme of life.

Show respect for all people, treat them honorably,
love the brotherhood of believers,
fear God, and honor the king.
1 Peter 2:17

Scan the QR code below to hear and save the emphasized message in this chapter.

Take a Risk

"Great things never came from comfort zones."
Anonymous

I've known and talked to many student-athletes who have told me that they didn't want to try out for one of our sports teams for one reason or another. I've even had a couple state they were afraid of how others would treat them if they didn't make the team.

It's always sad to see people with potential or something to offer a team, sit back, watch and never try out for a sport or other opportunities offered because they are afraid of being in the public eye or because they don't want to risk either losing or being embarrassed.

I'm most perplexed when I see the same students attending games in the sport they are purportedly interested in, laughing at the mishaps or jeering at the scholar athletes, who are doing their best while taking part in those sports.

In regards to these students, I often think: What will they risk to achieve success in their future? Will they always just want to stay comfortable? Will they always be envious of others who are trying? Will they take a chance to advance, even if it is hard? I pose the same questions to you.

I have found, when you carry a risk-averse attitude, you think more about what you will lose when you are trying something out of your comfort zone rather than what you will gain by taking the risk.

The real truth is, you cannot score in any sport if you never take a shot at the basket or goal. I also believe you never lose or fail at anything in life, you only gain lessons from the failures and struggles so you can learn, improve, and try your best to reach your potential.

The greatest basketball player of all time, Michael Jordan, shared, "I've missed more than nine thousand shots in my career. I've lost almost three hundred games. Twenty-six times, I've been trusted to take the game-winning shot and missed. I've failed over and over and over again in my life and that is why I succeed."

Personally, I've failed on many occasions. I've flopped at business ventures, career choices, relationships, and much more. Fortunately, I recognized from my missteps and defeats what success looks and feels like from my standpoint, not someone else or the masses.

You never fail if you try to do your best with the most positive intentions in mind. As a student-athlete or as a prospective student-athlete, when you finally step out and try out for the team, to become class president or any venture you set your sights on, you have to do so knowing if it doesn't work out, you will grow positively from it.

Do not be anxious about anything, but in every situation,
by prayer and petition, with thanksgiving,
present your requests to God.

And the peace of God, which transcends all understanding,
will guard your hearts and your minds in Christ Jesus.
Philippians 4:6-7

Scan the QR code below to hear and save
the highlighted theme in this chapter.

Enthusiasm can make a difference

"Nothing great was ever achieved without enthusiasm."
Ralph Waldo Emerson, American philosopher

I walked out of the tunnel with my teammates and sat in the chairs situated on the side of the court as Hall of Famer and the 19th ranked Kansas Jayhawks Head Basketball Coach, Larry Brown, was sitting with his hands outstretched, positive, and relaxed as they started to conclude their shootaround. I remember him confidently chatting with his players, including perennial All American, Danny Manning, laughing and having a good ol' time.

I was sitting about 25 feet away, paying attention and was pretty hyped up as my teammates and I knew that evening, the time to shine was upon us. It was the talk of the town, not only did the game have in-state rivalry implications, but pitted two head coaches who hailed from the University of North Carolina and were considered "Dean's Disciples," going head to head. Our coaches, Eddie Fogler and Larry Brown, played and/or coached alongside legendary coach Dean Smith before leaving the roost to start their own coaching legacies.

When game time came, we were ready! We came out of the tunnel, encircled the court and started our warmups. I remember jumping so high that one of my teammates, Steve Grayer, said, "Dang Beastie," as some of the fellas called me,

"Relax man, you might jump out of the gym!" I laughed.

The buzzer sounded to start the game and the packed house of 10,000 fans screamed continually throughout the game as both teams went back and forth, in a tight matchup. Ultimately, we were victorious and the arena went nuts!

Although I didn't play in this matchup, I clearly remember our film session the day after the big win. We always reviewed the game video to go over the highlights and lowlights, so coach could point out the good points and the mistakes made during the contest.

As we watched the film, Coach Fogler said, "Wow! Rewind that. Do you see what I see!" People quietly wondered what he was talking about. He said, "Look at that bench! Who is that, Teddy, Brent and John?" Someone answered, "Yes." He said give them each "6 plus points!" He continued, "Do you see the enthusiasm they are showing? That's what we need!" He was talking about how the three of us got into the game by cheering, chest bumping and having some fun when we (the team) did well. From then on, that was our thing. We had a routine fans came to expect. After games, people would sometimes say they were impressed with how we support our teammates and school although we don't play as many minutes. To be honest, it was not a position any of us ever wanted to be in, however we made the best of it. We had fun.

As you play basketball or other sports, your demeanor means a great deal to your coach, whether it's your attitude when coach takes you out of the game, or if you must come off the bench.

No coach wants to look down the pine (the bench) and see

or hear any player shaking his or her head side to side, sucking their teeth, on their cell phone, talking to their friends, leaning back in their chair, or worse, with their legs crossed or hands behind their head as the rest of the team competes. You must understand your body language and watch it closely. It says a lot about who you are and your attitude in that moment.

I've seen and heard it time and time again at all levels I've coached on. Players, about five games into the season, run into my office and complain about not playing enough, being taken out of a game or only playing a few minutes. It's so commonplace. I respond, "I notice on the bench, you look like you are uninterested in the game; it looks like someone just stole your lunch." It's always the same refrain, "It's the coach!" I go on to tell them that I'm quite sure this lack of enthusiasm for the team shows up in practice also. It's a vicious cycle.

You want to play more, but you don't want to work and sacrifice to do so. You only want the glory of playing, but don't want to uplift others as they shoot for success. The fact that you are not playing continually shows up in your attitude and demeanor and coaches detest that. Since the coach sits you more, the more peeved you (and likely your family) become until you explode and quit, storm out of practice, never to return, or you call your parents to meet with the coach.

Trust me, I learned. It's tough playing only five minutes a game and then lifting up your teammates and being as enthusiastic about their success as you would your own. You become a true hero and show great character when you can support others in achieving goals and help them get the most out of their ability.

What good is it to be frustrated about not playing more or coming out of the game? You don't control that. The most important thing is to always be ready! Even as you cheer on your teammates, you never know when you'll get the opportunity to shine but be content knowing that if your time never comes, you gave your best effort and showed enthusiasm every day in practice, in games, and maybe even from the pine.

"You are the light of the world.
A city set on a hill cannot be hidden.
Nor do people light a lamp and put it under a basket,
but on a stand, and it gives light to all in the house.
In the same way, let your light shine before others,
so that they may see your good works
and give glory to your Father who is in heaven.
Matthew 5:14-16

Scan the QR code below to hear and save the emphasized theme in this chapter.

Inner Competition

"Hard work beats talent when talent doesn't work hard."
Kevin Durant, American professional basketball player

One bright sunny summer day in 1999, I was sitting in my mom's living room and I wasn't feeling particularly well. I had negative thoughts racing through my mind with regards to stressful issues I was having or had confronted. It was such a disturbing condition that the back of my skull was actually pulsating.

I finally came to the realization that I had battled these thoughts before and I needed help. I called my best friend Nicole Sharpe and asked her if she could recommend someone I could talk to, because my mind just was not right. Although the call I eventually made to the psychologist was the toughest phone call I ever had to make, it became the most beneficial call I made in my life.

Prior to talking with and then meeting with the psychologist, I felt if I couldn't handle the concerns I had in my mind, that I was not a strong person. Thankfully, by reaching out for help by a trained professional, who provided me with the care I needed, I learned I was wrong.

I ascertained through this experience and other ordeals I've gone through, that we all will face competitors in life. As a student-athlete the challengers you face will vary. There is the rival that you can clearly see and interact with on the playing surface as you compete for positions, the best grades, or in trying to win games.

There are others, however, that you might engage that hinder your growth and development. These foes may be on the inside, in the form of your own thought life or beliefs. Specifically, the way you talk to yourself, how you see your future, the past, and what you are capable of. There is a potentially lengthy list of self-limiting thoughts you've adopted.

Some thoughts you may speak to yourself might be, "I suck," "I will never be happy," "I'm not attractive," "I'll never make the team," "I'm too skinny," "I'll never be able to speak in public," "I'll never be good enough," or even arrogantly, "I'm better than everyone".

You may wonder where these internal voices come from. Is it from our families, teachers, friends, heredity, failing tests, playing on losing teams, society, being raised in a poor, broken or even a rich household?

Circumstances you face in life affect how you see and speak to yourself. There are many positives you could reflect on, but most people probably keep negative influences or thoughts on the top of their mind.

Over time, if you don't find a way to dump these ideas, they build up, can weigh you down, and eventually drown out or dull any positive experiences you can have or know.

What delayed my seeking help sooner was the respites of relief I would get. For some unbeknownst reason, I'd get a day or two of relief from stress, worry or negative self-talk, and briefly break out of the slump. When the slump subsided,

I would have a vibrant day or weekend, but I would revert to the cycle once again. I could be caught up in that cycle for days, weeks or months and the light I really wanted to shine, would get extinguished.

Perhaps you, like many young people around you, don't feel like there is a way out of worry, depression, and anxiety. Many youths learn about, and seek temporary relief from, their issues by turning to drugs, alcohol, and sometimes hurt themselves through permanent solutions, like suicide, for problems that very likely have a resolution and are temporary.

Remember the lessons you have received as a student-athlete while playing individual or team sports. Recall relying on your coach to correct you when you made mistakes and relied on the entire team working in unison to get over obstacles to win contests.

Sometimes, when you have problems in life, you need a team to help you. The help of a professional or others can help you navigate to victory when facing opponents you can't see physically, but are there, nonetheless.

Below are ways that helped me recover from what I thought was endless anxiety:

(This should not take the place of seeking professional help.)

1. Reach out for help. Find a trusted person like a parent, guardian, counselor, school principal, guidance counselor, school psychologist or a sports coach. They are great resources to ask for help and to guide you with the support you will need. I still use a Christian counselor and psychologist to help counsel me through tough times I encounter in life.

2. Pray. If you have never prayed about your issue, know that God is alive and well and he answers prayers. What works for me is memorizing biblical scriptures that deal directly with an issue and I repeat it whenever my thoughts go awry. When praying, you must be able to delay your gratification and patiently wait for the resolution, because God's answers may not come as fast as you would like.

3. Prune out the negatives in your life. This includes people who are negative. Turn off watching negative news and social media. Try reading uplifting books, videos, or articles, and surround yourself with positive/supportive people.

4. Understand that you can only control yourself and not much else. You cannot control other people, the world or what takes place in it. Take care of you.

5. Cut yourself some slack. Forgive others and yourself for past failures and things that did not go as planned or assumed. Create a positive self-talk script, positive affirmation or biblical verses to repeat to yourself when you start to think negatively.

6. Be here now. Relax, be patient, and live in the moment. Instead of thinking about what could have been or what is coming up, live life right now. Feel your breathing, the texture of this book you are holding, the air going in and out of your nose right now, the chair you are sitting on and the current sound you are hearing. Train your mind to be in every second.

7. Laugh. There is nothing like resolving negative thinking like reading a funny story or listening to a video or

comedian make fun of the silly things we do as humans every day.

8. Exercise. As an athlete, you are likely very aware of how much better you feel about life once you finish your workout in the pool, on the field or on the court. You feel this way because of the endorphins released in your body after exercise. They are natural mood enhancers. Keep up the training when you feel low, maybe not as intense, but moving your body by even walking on a nice day or evening helps tremendously.

9. Enjoy a hobby, like journaling, singing, writing, flying kites or model airplanes, reading, basketball, volleyball, riding bikes, hiking, fishing or podcasting (as I do) about a subject you enjoy. I podcast and write to express myself because I can't sing, make music or run up and down the court as often as I used to.

10. Socialize in person and specifically face to face with positive people, friends and influences, not just online or on your phone.

Finally, don't forget about all the good you've done, seen and experienced in life. As you grow older, there is a tendency to forget the positive list you can make right now. Reflect on the good grades, the funny stories, the blessings you've received from God, the trophies earned, the good health, the clothes, the food, the games, the safe home or the fact that you have people at school and at home that love you, rather than what you don't have or have lost.

For our struggle is not (really) against human opponents,
but against rulers, authorities,
cosmic powers in the darkness around us,
and evil spiritual forces in the heavenly realm.
Ephesians 6:12

Scan the QR code below to hear and save
the highlighted message in this chapter.

YOU ARE
MORE
THAN A
CONQUEROR!

BELIEVE IT!

Quotes are not enough

"Every morning in Africa, a gazelle wakes up,
it knows it must outrun the fastest lion
or it will be killed.
Every morning in Africa, a lion wakes up.
It knows it must run faster than the slowest gazelle,
or it will starve.
It doesn't matter whether you're the lion or a gazelle
when the sun comes up, you'd better be running."
Dan Montano, Securities analyst

When I was about 11 years old, my brother Kevin left the above quote on my bed. It is the first motivational quote I remember receiving, and after I read it, I was instantly inspired. I was so fascinated. I kept reading it over and over. It made so much sense, offered me a jolt of enthusiasm, and helped me to continue the discipline of getting up every dawn to workout.

Many athletes, coaches, and mentors are big on quotes, and self-guidance books they have read or written themselves. Coaches tend to post quotes throughout locker areas, paint weight rooms with them, give out inspirational writings on holidays for their teams to read, and start or end pregame and halftime speeches with them.

They do this so that the words can motivate you to strive for greatness individually, and for the team or sport you are playing on.

I have posted my fair share of self-help and motivational videos on podcasts, websites and my own social media accounts for others to see.

I've uncovered that using motivational expressions and self-help can help to keep us energized at the moment. Over time, however, they can lose their effect. I relate good self-help to a bag of barbeque chips; they satisfy for a few minutes or for an hour or so, but never wholly satisfy you, and leave you wanting more.

I've understood that what self-help can't resolve, God can. And unlike that bag of chips that doesn't really nourish you, God can truly satisfy you every day and for a lifetime, when you spend time praying to and praising The Creator.

I must admit, if I was at this point in the book during a certain point in my life as you may be, I would have a perplexed look. I would be wondering why God was being discussed; however, over time and through life's lessons, I realized I cannot live life bountifully by having quotes, videos and self-help to sustain me, but only through surrendering to God or the Holy Spirit.

As humans, we think we are so smart. Many of us, at certain points, think we can outwit God and only live on our own accord; it may work for a while, but never lasts, at least not for me and others who I've listened to and talked with about this topic.

I've determined every day, to turn my face to God, put on my spiritual armor in prayer before my feet hit the ground and to listen, read and meditate on various passages in the bible for a few minutes, ingesting it incrementally like a good meal. It is called spiritual nourishment.

As student-athletes, your coaches ask you to get stronger day by day by eating right to keep your frames durable to be the best player you can be. That's what you must do to get spiritually stronger day by day. You may be weak to start, but if you keep at it with patience, you will become more fortified as you grow in faith by ingesting the word of God (The Bible) and talking to God (praying) as you would your best friend, every day.

Trust me, there is no quote, tattoo, publication, television show, pastor, family member, philosophy, YouTube motivation, alcohol, drug, music, dance party, boyfriend, girlfriend, meditation, yoga, food, exercise, endorphins, interpretations or contraptions you can come up with that can give you freedom and peace of mind like the Creator.

Try God, and watch your performance both on and off the court improve.

For he satisfies the longing soul,

and the hungry soul he fills with good things.
Psalms 107:9

Scan the QR code below to hear and save
the emphasized theme in this chapter.

Rise Early

"Wake up early and tackle the day
before it tackles you.
Be on offense, not defense."
Evan Carmichael, Entrepreneur

Have you heard of the adage, "the early bird gets the worm?"

As a young man, watching the way my father and Kevin rose from bed early exemplified the habit for me. From my father, I understood the morning was a good opportunity for quiet contemplation, prayer, to prepare for work, and express care by preparing breakfast for his children. From Kevin, I grasped that getting up early was an occasion to work out, and to work toward reaching goals while most others were likely hitting the snooze button and just turning over in bed.

As a pre-teen, I began to discipline myself by rising early. I figured out that once I was able to get myself up, wash my face, and brush my teeth, I could muster up the energy easier than in the evening, to work productively on my basketball game. I would dress quickly, take my notepad drills I wrote describing the drills my youth coaches, Vincent Smith and my cousin Pierre showed me, and head to the park. I would shoot my three hundred jumpers, practice my two ball dribbling drills, and dream.

Once I began disciplining my body and mind to rise early, noticed that I felt much better physically and mentally. I ever felt better spiritually because I learned the early morning was the best time for me to communicate with God. I, of course became more positive about life in general than the days slept until the last minute before leaving for school or unti nine or ten o'clock in the morning on weekends. I realized this was a healthy lifestyle change and one that I still reap the benefits from every day.

"How long will you lie there, you sluggard?
When will you get up from your sleep?
A little sleep, a little slumber,
a little folding of the hands to rest and
poverty will come on you like a thief
and scarcity like an armed man."
Proverbs 6:9-11

Scan the QR code below to hear and save
the highlighted message in this chapter.

Balance

"Life is about balance; too much and too little can kill.
The best way to balance life is setting your boundaries
and learning to say enough."
M.G. Garcia, Commanding General, US Army

When I began to drive a car, sometimes after working out I would go for a ride to my favorite park in Irvington, NY, walk down to the local park, or just go to one of my friend's house to take some pressure I put on myself off. Striving to be the best basketball player left me feeling exhausted frequently.

Even today, although my college playing experience is long gone, I still give myself a regular break from my standard workout routine to do something different in order to relax and let my mental and physical body recover, before getting back into my workout regimen again.

As an athlete, when you are pursuing the goal or even as others push you hard to become a high school, college, or professional athlete, you must remember to take some time off to just chill. If you don't, you risk burnout, which can lead to disliking the sport you profess to love.

If you are a serious student-athlete nowadays, unfortunately, you likely started training seriously by the age of six or seven years old and playing not only locally, but even nationally in two or three games each weekend and practicing several times a week to be prepared all year-round! This incredible schedule leaves little time to just be a kid and to do much else other than schoolwork and looking at or posting to social media.

In comparison, during my pre-teen years, my friends and I honed our sports skills by playing together outside in the park or somebody's backyard by having fun emulating our sports heroes, creating our own moves; not with sports specific trainers, but with our imaginations.

When I reached my teens, I began to focus, train and refine my moves playing against friends in the park, working out and by playing in weekend tournaments; but only during the summer and winter months, not year-round. Even with this lighter schedule, at times I felt burned out from basketball and the pressure I felt to be the best.

When I suggest that you have to chill, I mean don't forget to have fun by taking part in doing things you enjoy or used to enjoy before sports-specific training or playing took over. Remember to be a kid and go to the movies, ride bikes, head to the go-cart track, play video games or even take a big leap and try out for a different sports team, like baseball instead of basketball or wrestling instead of soccer. This may mean telling your family or coach, no thank you, when they ask you where you want to sit in the plane for the upcoming 15 and under national tournament or what number you want to wear in the next travel league.

Loosen up and enjoy your youth, if you are not already! Understand that you build more strength when you let your mind, body and soul relax by taking a day or two off or trying something new. This simple act of choosing to unwind, may in fact, reignite your fire even more so for the sport that you love!

And be not conformed to this world;
but be ye transformed by the renewing of your mind,
that ye may prove what is the good,
and acceptable, and perfect, will of God.
Romans 12:2

Scan the QR code below to hear and save
the emphasized theme in this chapter.

You're Rich

"Rich people stay rich by living like they're broke.
Broke people stay broke by living like they're rich."
Avinash Wandre, Indian Philosopher and Teacher

———————————◆———————————

I grew up in this small working-class town called Elmsford, New York, about 20 miles from New York City. It was a town my friend Wayne Anderson called Utopia, or the perfect society.

Elmsford, New York, when I was growing up, was a place where almost all two thousand people knew each other. For the most part, people in our village got along and there were no big racial, economic, educational or religious divisions, as each family was working class, minded their own business, and lived in quaint half-acre homes.

The community was safe, and kids individually and collectively, could frolic all day riding bikes, shooting hoops, walking to church, partying at block parties, playing softball, marching in parades, and always kept busy playing in the youth baseball, basketball and football programs. It was non-stop fun!

One sunny late afternoon, when I was about nine, I was walking home from the playground, planning to stop at Lewis's corner store. My older brother Wayne, who was headed in the opposite direction, stopped me and uttered,

'What's up?"

 mumbled, "What's up?"

He said, "I want to tell you something."

'Ok, what's going on?" I asked.

 As I listened, he simply said, "We're not rich."

I went, "Huh?"

"We're not rich!" he repeated.

I remember quizzically wondering to myself, "What is this dude talking about?"

He must've read my mind because he commented, "We're barely making it bro! We're what you call, lower middle class. We think that we're rich but we're actually on the verge of being poor. Mommy and Daddy provide everything we need, like food, clothes, shoes, family vacations and all types of stuff and make us feel like we're rich, but if Mommy or Daddy did not both work, we'd be poor."

I remember thinking, "wow," as he walked to the park and I continued to the store. I eventually figured Wayne must have learned something new by watching the news that night.

What I do know, is that conversation resonated with me. After thinking our conversation from that point on, I remember looking at life with a slightly different perspective, particularly how we were raised and what we attained. I became more thoughtful about what I begged my parents to buy. I also realized that although we may not have been rich monetarily, we were rich in ways others were not.

Today, most people believe that striving to make money to acquire more things, means you are rich. The by-product of buying these items is that others give you recognition for the things you have, which is unfortunate. Students from all backgrounds – and adults – I know and have had conversations with believe if they get more cars, clothes, shoes, toys or stuff, it will make them happy and others will accept them as being cool.

Many call this condition "Keeping up with the Joneses." People seek the attention of neighbors and others they know by buying stuff to impress them. Once they are impressed with your stuff, they then go out and buy something, to try and impress you and it never stops. How silly is this?

Student-athletes fall into this trap, by not only trying to possess material items, but unlike those who are not athletes, many try to maintain the status and adoration of people who cheered you on throughout your playing days.

As an athlete you become so familiar with the attention, you continually seek validation from others as you move forward, whether on the court or off it. You have developed a big EGO, or should I say, a certain level of self-importance that you thrive on.

What happens when the cheering stops for good one day? Will you feel fulfilled and rich? Have you considered that the continual praise you get for your stellar performances now will be far in the past one day?

I've learned the real riches in life come from the inside: your mindset, your spirit, from God; not from outside things you own or from cheering fans. Wouldn't you prefer to be alone, healthy and content rather than looking for others to tell you how great you are?

I know people who have, and had, plenty of money and can

buy things like excursions to distant lands who are angry, ornery and oftentimes negative, especially when they or the things they own are not fawned over by others. They are empty inside.

How will you fill the void when you aren't the talk of the town and you are not feeling particularly popular anymore? Do you buy more stuff or enter the keeping up with the Joneses game to get temporary relief? Or do you turn to drinking or drugs?

Maybe, just maybe, you have developed a crack in your foundation, as I found in myself. If you do, let me tell you, you can dig deep beneath the misery and find something (just one thing) to help you start to dig out of your hole of seeking the acceptance of others.

It will take work and a substantial amount of effort and energy. I'd like to help you out by offering four ways you can try to uplift yourself and feel rich, without money or admiration from others outside of you, but from the inside out.

1) You can be overflowing with spiritual health by having an intimate connection to God. Develop trust in the Holy Spirit and understanding there is a positive plan for your life and your own personal story or testimony that can serve others. Learn to live in the now, not the past or the future.

2) You can be rich with a good attitude, learning to look at people from a perspective of who they are rather than what they own or who they know. As a matter of fact, I have taught children in schools who are considered homeless with some of the best attitudes!

3) You can try to abound with physical health, by understanding eating poorly (including fast food) only makes

you feel better because as a young child you were trained to put food in your mouth to help soothe your pain. The best long-term decision for your body, brain and emotions is purchasing fruits and vegetables which are more bountiful in nutrients, are cheaper in price, and much healthier for you.

4) You can be prosperous with mental and emotional health by decreasing the negativity surrounding you from people, social media, your phone and television. If necessary, seek help from trusted people or professionals if you need to discuss any troubling thoughts.

In the health class I teach, when we are studying maintaining good overall health, I tell my students, "Although having money is an important aspect of life, if you cannot be healthy mentally, spiritually, physically, and emotionally also, you can have all the money you want, you still won't be happy."

As they look at me quizzically I state, "I believe life is about the quality of life not the quantity of life or the number or things you own. Why would you want to live a long life with a lot of money, but not be healthy enough to enjoy it? I'd rather live a long life, with good and balanced health, and be content with what I have and can do."

How about you?

One pretends to be rich, yet has nothing;
another pretends to be poor, yet has great wealth.
Proverbs 13:7

————————➤

Scan the QR code below to hear and save
the highlighted message in this chapter.

Bonus Chapter

"Carpe Diem"
(Seize the Day)

Think of the days you've let slip by
A beautiful sunset or a clear blue sky

For time is a treasure for all to share
we should treat every second as if it were rare

Cherish each moment with all of your heart
be excited in knowing it's a brand-new start

Every day's an opportunity for us to grow
being a warm special person is all we should know

For those wasting time with anger and hate
the future will bestow an unenviable fate

Chose to see the good in all that's before you
The choice is yours, it's what you must do

Why have others passed on and you still remain?
the answer is easy, your life's not in vain

Look straight ahead at what you'll achieve
the secret of each moment is that you believe

Believe in the Lord and He'll set you free
and the wonders of life will be yours to see

Phil Weber
Longtime NBA Coach, Motivational Speaker, Poet

Thank you for reading BasSketball Lessons!

I would really appreciate your feedback and would love to read what you have to say. Your input will help me make the next version of this book and my future books better.

Leaving a helpful review of the book on Amazon.com and letting me know what you thought of the book would be awesome!

Also, leave me a note by going to
www.BasSketballLessons.com and scrolling to the "Contact" section at the very bottom of the page and **I'll send you the companion resource guide for free!**

Thank you so much!!!!

~ Brent Bass

Made in the USA
Coppell, TX
15 January 2023

11147236R00056